Candice & Edgar
Bergen

by

Skip Press

CRESTWOOD HOUSE

Parsippany, New Jersey

Library of Congress Cataloging-in-Publication Data
Press, Skip, 1950–
    Candice & Edgar Bergen / by Skip Press. — 1st ed.
        p.   cm. — (Star families)
    ISBN 0-89686-878-8   pbk 0-382-24940-2
    1. Bergen, Candice, 1946–   —Juvenile literature. 2. Bergen, Edgar, 1903–1978—Juvenile literature. 3. Actors—United
States—Biography—Juvenile literature. 4. Ventriloquists—United States—Biography—Juvenile literature. [1. Bergen,
Candice, 1946– 2. Actors and actresses. 3. Women—Biography. 4. Bergen, Edgar, 1903–1978. 5. Ventriloquists.] I. Title.
II. Title: Candice and Edgar Bergen. III. Series.
PN2287.B434P74   1995
792'.02'092273—dc20
[B]   94-20395
    Summary: The life story of comedic actress Candice Bergen and her famous ventriloquist father, Edgar Bergen.

Photo Credits
All photos courtesy of AP—Wide World Photos.

Acknowledgments
The author would like to thank the following people for their contributions in compiling this book:
David Sheff and *Playboy* magazine; Jim Jerome, Sue Carswell, Sabrina McFarland, and *People* magazine; David Ragan and
Cosmopolitan magazine; John F. Ross and *Smithsonian* magazine; the National Recording Company of Glenview, Illinois;
Nancy Turner and Peeter Alvet; Ephraim Katz, author of *The Film Encyclopedia*; the magnificent staff of the Margaret Herrick
Library at the Academy of Motion Picture Arts and Sciences; Edgar Bergen, author of *How To Become A Ventriloquist*; and,
most of all, Candice Bergen, author of *Knock Wood*.

Published by Crestwood House, an imprint of Silver Burdett Press,
A Simon & Schuster Company
299 Jefferson Road, Parsippany, NJ 07054

Produced by Great Flying Fish/Spicer, MN

Printed in the United States of America

10 9 8 7 6 5 4 3 2 1

Contents

Candice Bergen has made her mark as an actress through her role as Murphy Brown.

Thank You, Dan Quayle

In September 1992, Vice President Dan Quayle spoke to an audience that included film and television star Candice Bergen. With a wry smile, he turned to the famous actress and said, "Now, Murphy Brown, listen closely because I'm only going to say it once. You owe me big time."

The wisecrack drew a huge laugh. Candice Bergen laughed, too, all the way to the bank. Quayle's comment was directed toward the fictional character Candice Bergen played on TV. The ratings of her popular, award-winning show, *Murphy Brown*, had been soaring since an earlier Quayle comment. In that earlier speech, the vice president had remarked on Murphy Brown's decision to become an unwed mother. Making that choice seemed okay on TV, he suggested, but sent the wrong message to the country's youth.

The vice president was merely promoting what he considered appropriate family values. He had meant to say that it would set a better example if TV characters who had babies got married first. The simple remark had set off a firestorm of protest in Hollywood. "Censorship!" cried Diane English, the creator and producer of *Murphy Brown*. English saw the vice president's comment as a personal, politically motivated attack. Candice Bergen made similar statements. Supporters of Candice Bergen and of the vice president were each defending their "hero." After all, many of the leading lights of Hollywood were **Democrats**, while the **Republicans**—including Quayle—governed in Washington.

The battle of ideas between *Murphy Brown* and Dan Quayle was still going strong later in 1992 when Bergen accepted the

Emmy Award for outstanding lead actress in a comedy series. She told her audience: "I would like to thank the vice president and I would like to thank the television academy and members of the cultural elite."

The cast of *Murphy Brown* from right to left: Charles Kimbrough, Candice Bergen, Joe Regalbuto, Faith Ford, and Grant Shaud

It didn't stop there. In May 1993 Candice Bergen accepted the sixteenth annual **Jack Benny Award** from the University of California at Los Angeles (UCLA). The award is given for excellence in comedy. In accepting her award, Bergen jokingly told the audience that the "Quayle episode" was a significant political experience in the history of the country.

Not long after Democrat Bill Clinton became President of the United States in January 1993, he told the press that Quayle had been right. The country *did* need better family values, Clinton said. By then, the uproar had died down. Quayle was no longer in office, but *Murphy Brown* was still going strong. Diane English no longer produced the show, but Murphy's trademark sharp remarks were still as biting as ever.

To anyone who knew the story of Candice Bergen, her involvement in a media flurry over sharp remarks was nothing new. Ironically, in the past it had been Candice making the wisecracks. With the Quayle incident, it was someone else commenting about *her* that made the news.

Candice admitted in her 1984 autobiography *Knock Wood* that the smart mouth she was famous for was simply a defense. She made smart-aleck comments about people and things out of her own insecurity, she said. But who could blame her for using the device? After all, she had grown up as the "sister" of one of the biggest smart alecks in entertainment history.

The name of her "brother" was Charlie McCarthy, and he was a wooden **dummy**. Charlie came to life courtesy of Candice's father, the **ventriloquist** Edgar Bergen. For over 50 years, Edgar and Charlie amused and delighted stage, radio, film, and television audiences with their unique brand of humor. Wisecracking Charlie was so loved by the public that when Candice was born, newspapers and magazines called her "Charlie's sister." Reporters even made an issue of the fact that Charlie's room at the Bergen home was larger than baby Candice's nursery.

Actually, major media focus on the children of famous stars was normal in those days. As an example, Candice's pet turtle died when Candice was six. Of course, such an event is important in a child's life, but the turtle's funeral—in the Bergens' Beverly Hills backyard—was covered by the *Saturday Evening Post*! Though Candice was at the forefront of the article, the *Post* was interested only because of Edgar Bergen and Charlie McCarthy.

Still, because of her beauty and talent, Candice might have become a show business success even without a famous father and an immensely popular "brother." Although she got a big head start as Edgar Bergen's daughter, she resisted doing comedy for many years—despite her father's encouragement. In fact, when she first auditioned for the part of Murphy Brown, few people thought she was right for it. After several years in the role, though, it was hard to imagine her doing anything *but* comedy.

Edgar Bergen gave his daughter a rich heritage of humor, and she made the best of it. That heritage began long ago, when a form of traveling variety show called **vaudeville** was the most popular entertainment in the world.

Candice wins an Emmy Award for her comedic role as Murphy Brown.

The Story of Charlie McCarthy

Edgar John Berggren was born in Michigan on February 16, 1903, to Swedish immigrant dairy farmers named John and Nell Berggren. Edgar was the Berggrens' younger son. His older brother was named Clarence.

Edgar was a bright, inquisitive boy. When he was 11 years old, he paid 25¢ for a book called *The Wizard's Manual*. The mail-order book was filled with beginning magic tricks, including

Edgar Bergen with his two famous sidekicks, Charlie McCarthy (*left*) and Mortimer P. Snerd (*right*) in 1938

ventriloquism. The word *ventriloquism* comes from two Latin words: *venter*, meaning "stomach," and *loquor*, meaning "to speak." Thus the word actually means "speaking from the stomach (or belly)," although ventriloquism is often called "throwing your voice." The ventriloquist's words seem to come not from his or her lips but from another object. Edgar first used "belly talking" to scare his mother. In the kitchen one day, he made her think an apple pie was talking to her! Her reaction convinced him that he was onto something amazing.

In the early 1900s, "belly talkers," also known as "vents," were the least respected of vaudeville performers. Edgar dreamed of being a vaudeville magician but continued to be fascinated with the art of ventriloquism.

When Edgar was 16, his father died. Edgar's mother, Nell, moved the family from Michigan to Decatur, Illinois. Clarence went to work as an apprentice accountant, while Edgar worked part-time in a silent-movie house. He continued to practice magic and ventriloquism. Near the movie house where he worked, a redheaded boy named Charlie sold newspapers on the street. Charlie was a talkative, likeable lad who wore a sweater and knitted cap in cold weather. As Edgar revealed in his book, *How to Become a Ventriloquist*, the newsboy "spoke in the slangy, careless words of a boy who had to make his own way in the world."

To make his ventriloquism more lifelike, Edgar decided to create a dummy. Charlie became Edgar's model for the dummy. Edgar made sketches, then paid a bartender named Mack $35 to carve a pine head of "Charlie." Edgar made the rest of the dummy himself and dressed it to look like the newsboy. He named the dummy Charlie McCarthy, after the newsboy and the woodcarving bartender. Edgar's first public outing with Charlie McCarthy was in Chicago at an amateur performance that paid $5 a night. Edgar's act featured both magic and ventriloquism. The manager hired him but insisted that Edgar cut out the magic and shorten his name to the more easily pronounced Bergen. Edgar agreed and spent the next summer on a vaudeville tour as a working "vent."

To his mother's great relief, Edgar decided that he wanted to become a doctor. After graduating from high school, he enrolled in Northwestern University as a premed student. He continued performing with Charlie to help pay his way through college. Later he transferred to the school of speech but never graduated. Show business was calling, quite loudly.

Edgar and Charlie headed off on the Sawdust Trail—as vaudeville was called—playing across the country for the next ten years. They became so popular that, in 1930, they were invited to perform at the Palace, a theater at 47th Street and **Broadway** in New York City where no lowly ventriloquist had ever performed. The Palace was the greatest theater in the country. It regularly featured top acts like singer Al Jolson, escape artist Harry Houdini, the hilarious Marx Brothers, and the dancing Astaires (Fred and his sister Adele).

For two years Bergen was the top ventriloquist in vaudeville. The country's mood was changing, however. Movies now had sound, and radio shows were increasingly popular. But what really killed vaudeville was something more serious. The nation was in the midst of a severe economic crisis. In 1932 the Palace, that great dream of vaudeville performers, was forced to close for lack of business. Vaudeville was dead. Edgar redesigned his act

12   Edgar created this life-sized character, Miss Podine Puffington, in 1950.

to save it. He and Charlie dressed up in tuxedos and top hats. Charlie began to wear a monocle—an eyeglass in one eye—so he would appear to be more sophisticated.

Charlie may have *looked* refined, but he didn't talk that way. The words out of his mouth, like Charlie the newsboy's, were still snappy and streetwise. Audiences loved the contrast in the way Charlie looked and the way he spoke. Bergen and McCarthy played expensive supper clubs, like Chicago's Chez Paree. Noël Coward, a well-known playwright and composer, saw them perform and got them a booking at New York's Rainbow Room.

Their appearance at this prestigious supper club led to the biggest break of all. From the Rainbow Room Edgar and his wooden costar landed a spot on the *Fleischmann Hour*, a radio show starring the singer Rudy Vallee. So in 1936 Bergen and McCarthy traveled to Los Angeles to do their first radio show.

By the 1930s, radio was the most popular form of entertainment in the world, with great impact on the performers' careers. For example, Bob Hope, Bing Crosby, Jack Benny, and Burns and Allen (George Burns and his wife, Gracie Allen) were all radio personalities who went on to star in films.

Part of the humor of Bergen and McCarthy's spot on the Vallee show was that the radio audience couldn't *see* them. Even though they performed before a live audience in the studio, the people listening at home couldn't tell whether or not Bergen's lips moved while speaking as Charlie. But it worked. Charlie's snappy exchanges with Bergen were a big hit. After two more appearances on the Vallee show, they got their own show. It was *The Chase and Sanborn Hour*, named after their coffee company sponsors.

When vaudeville faded in popularity, Edgar changed Charlie's look from a newsboy to a gentleman with a tuxedo, top hat, and monocle.

By 1938 Bergen and McCarthy's Sunday-evening show was the most widely heard radio program in America. They were already film stars. Between 1933 and 1935 Edgar and Charlie had appeared in a dozen film shorts for the Vitaphone Company. And in 1937 Edgar received a special **Academy Award** for *creating* Charlie McCarthy. No entertainers in America were more popular than Bergen and McCarthy.

Film stars were frequent guests on their radio program. The comedian W. C. Fields—whose nose was red and inflamed from drinking too much alcohol—often feuded with Charlie on the air. When Fields threatened to "sic a beaver" on Charlie, the wooden dummy quipped: "Mr. Fields, is that a flame thrower I see, or is it your nose?"

Edgar introduced new characters on the radio show, such as Mortimer Snerd, the dumbest dummy ever invented. "You certainly have more than your share of stupidity," Edgar remarked to Mortimer. "It's the old story," Mortimer replied. "Them who has, gets." But no character was as popular as Charlie McCarthy, or came even close.

In 1938 Edgar moved to Bel Air, a rich community not far from Beverly Hills, California. He bought a house named Bella Vista and brought his mother out to live with him. Edgar stayed busy. In addtion to the radio show, he and his wooden creations appeared in feature films, such as *You Can't Cheat an Honest Man* (with W.C. Fields) and *Charlie McCarthy, Detective* (both in 1939). Bergen seemed content to spend his free time at home, practicing his old magic tricks. He was referred to as "the most eligible bachelor in Hollywood" but didn't seem to care. That all changed the night Edgar met Frances Westerman.

Charlie's Sister
and the Magic Kingdom

After her husband, William, died of tuberculosis, Lillie Mae Westerman moved from Birmingham, Alabama, to Los Angeles, California. Frances, her 10-year old daughter, was heartbroken. Her father had been the light of her life. Lillie Mae remarried, but her new husband was always out of work. The marriage didn't last long. Lillie Mae supported herself and Frances, struggling through their troubles somehow. To cheer 14-year-old Frances up after she was involved in an auto accident, Lillie Mae gave her a Charlie McCarthy doll.

By the time Frances graduated from Los Angeles High School, she was tall and beautiful. She worked as a model for the I. Magnin department store, earning her own money. When Frances was 19, a show staff member invited her to see *The Edgar Bergen Show with Charlie McCarthy*. Frances sat in the front row. Edgar, 39 at the time, spotted Frances from the stage. After the show, he asked to meet her. Soon, the most eligible bachelor in Hollywood had fallen in love.

When Frances moved to New York to pursue her modeling career, Edgar courted her there. He watched as she became "the Chesterfield girl" for a cigarette company, appearing in print ads and on roadside billboards. He continued dating her when she became "the Ipana girl" for a toothpaste company.

Frances fell in love, too. In June 1945 she and Edgar married in a small ceremony in Mexico. The headline of the *Los Angeles Herald Examiner* proclaimed: "CHARLIE GETS STEPMOTHER." Frances was 20 years old. Her husband was twice her age.

Less than a year later, Charlie got a sister. On May 9, 1946, 7-pound, 13½-ounce Candice was born at Hollywood Presbyterian Hospital. Charlie's room at Bella Vista, with a view of the rose garden and an entrance off the patio, became the nursery. The velvet-lined trunk where Charlie "slept" was placed in the guest room next door.

The Bergen house was at the top of a mountain, surrounded by a rose garden, wild flowers, and exotic trees and shrubs. With her Dutch **governess**, Dena, known as Dee, watching out for her, young Candy began exploring her hillside surroundings as soon as possible. Further up the mountain, she discovered the old John Barrymore estate. Candice was enchanted by one of the houses on the estate known as the Aviary. The famous actress Katharine Hepburn lived there.

"To me," Candice Bergen said in *Knock Wood*, "Bella Vista was like a **Magic Kingdom**."

Part of the magic might have been Walt Disney, who lived nearby. The creator of Mickey Mouse, Donald Duck, and Disneyland took Candice and her parents for train rides on the miniature steam engine in his backyard. "Uncle Walt" was the engineer. When Walt appeared on Edgar's show in 1947 with Mickey Mouse and Donald Duck, it was to promote *Fun and Fancy Free*, a Disney film costarring Edgar and Charlie. The Bergens saw all the new Disney films in Walt's screening room, before they were released to the public. For Candice's sixth birthday party, Walt screened his *Snow White* for her and her friends (it later became an animated classic). The film made quite an impression on the young girl.

Edgar and Francis Bergen pose with five-week-old Candice as Charlie McCarthy looks on.

19

The age of six also marked Candice's debut as a professional entertainer, when she appeared on her father's Christmas show.

"Tonight Candy's going to be on this show and that's why I'm so happy," Bergen told his radio audience. "You know," he confided to Charlie, "she's the apple of my eye."

"Yes, of course," replied a jealous Charlie, "but don't forget, I'm the cabbage of your bankbook."

"I recited my well-learned lines with considerable poise and polish," Candice Bergen said in her book, "a perfect little ham, a wind-up doll—a dummy. A daughter determined to make good."

The public loved Candy. She was invited back for the Easter show. In one skit she and Charlie went on an Easter egg hunt in the **Enchanted Forest**.

Candy and Charlie sent wisecracks back and forth between each other during the skit. The audience found their act to be hilarious. When the laughter died down, Charlie announced, "I'm beginning to like this girl!"

Edgar Bergen had one passion other than magic—flying. In his spare time, he liked to pilot his private plane to his family's house in Palm Springs, or to the Grand Canyon, or Yosemite National Park. Frances hated flying—it made her ill. She got her pilot's license as a wedding gift to Edgar, but she avoided being in the air unless absolutely necessary. Candy, however, loved any chance to spend time alone with her ventriloquist father, who breathed life "into blocks of wood, sending blood through lifeless glass-eyed bodies." She was his fairy princess. "Known and loved wherever we went," she recalled. "Flying and famous . . . Like God, sort of, or Superman, it seemed to me then."

Candice loved spending time with her father as a young girl and seemed to have a natural ability as a performer.

Edgar had a great passion for flying and traveled by air whenever possible.

Was the Bergen house really a magic kingdom? Well, consider the Christmas party at Bella Vista the year Candice was 13. The Jimmy Stewarts, the Ronald Reagans, and other celebrities were there. Fred Astaire danced with Candice's mother. Rex Harrison sang from *My Fair Lady*, the musical he starred in. At the piano was the world-famous Henry Mancini, and Santa Claus looked remarkably like the legendary actor David Niven.

Perhaps because Candy spent so much time in the company of sophisticated adults, she was mature beyond her years. She learned how much so the hard way. Her parents owned a house in Newport Beach, which they visited on the weekends. One Sunday, a famous young blond-haired actor sailed up with some of the Bergens' friends. Candy was amazed. In typical teenage fashion, she had a poster of the actor on her bedroom wall! The actor took her sailing and asked her for a secret date. The next Wednesday, with her parents out of town, Candy sneaked out of her house without the housekeeper's finding out.

The actor was not her **Prince Charming**, she discovered. He drove Candice to a secluded spot and tried to pressure her into doing things she was definitely not ready for. Frustrated by her childish behavior, the actor drove her home immediately.

The incident convinced Candy that she needed to get away from the fast lane of life in Hollywood. She convinced her parents to send her to a private girls' school in Gstaad, Switzerland. Little did she know it, but she was jumping from a barely sizzling frying pan into a very hot European fire.

Not Exactly A Model Student

To put it mildly, the Montesano School was not the safe haven Candy imagined it to be. When she arrived, Montesano had 65 students from around the world. They were, as she put it, "the aristocrats of abandoned children—chic semi-orphans begging for discipline, desperate for love." Every girl, it seemed, was much more worldly than Candice. Drinking and smoking were the "cool" things to do at Montesano—an extreme contrast to life in Bel Air. The preferred language was French, which was no problem for Candy. The life-style of the students became a problem for her, though, when her parents showed up for Christmas. They found she had bleached her hair, was smoking cigarettes, and drank alcoholic beverages whenever she wanted.

Montesano lasted one term for Candy. She went home, surprised at how relieved she was to be there. Another surprise awaited her as well. On October 12, 1961, Candice became a big sister, when Frances Bergen gave birth to Kris Edgar Bergen. The new arrival brought the family closer together.

"My mother radiated a new sense of serenity," Candice said, "and my father, at sixty, was born again with his new boy. For me, it was the beginning of a bond of such depth and intensity that I was often baffled by it, overwhelmed by the love I felt."

Before leaving for Switzerland, Candy had often been expelled from classes with her wisecracking friend Connie Frieberg. Reunited, they returned to their old prankster ways, but caused no major trouble. The rest of Candy's high-school years were fairly normal—at least as normal as they could be, attending the private Westlake School in Bel Air.

At 16, she fell in love for the first time. The boy was Terry Melcher, the son of the movie star Doris Day. He was 20 years old, had quit college, and was working for Columbia Records. Blond-haired, blue-eyed Terry had "a touch of Tom Sawyer about him in spirit as well as looks—a taste for tricks and trouble, an instinct for truth." Like Candy.

Candy was elected May Queen at her high school that year, but her youthful popularity didn't satisfy Terry. He broke up with her to date 24-year-old singer Jackie de Shannon. Candy was crushed at losing him.

When it came time for college, Candy chose the University of Pennsylvania. The Ivy League school had a beautiful campus far from Hollywood. It also had three boys for every girl. In her first semester there, Candy was elected Homecoming Queen. *The Philadelphia Inquirer* newspaper headline declared "CHARLIE'S SISTER HOMECOMING QUEEN—NO DUMMY SHE." As Miss University of Pennsylvania, she was asked to escort Republican presidential candidate Barry Goldwater onstage for a speech. That was the extent of her political activity at the time.

Candice poses for the cameras after being named Miss University of Pennsylvania in 1963.

At college Candy discovered the work of Margaret Bourke-White, the most famous female **photojournalist** in the world. She met Mary Ellen Mark, a photography student who would become a lifelong friend. On the other side of the camera, at the end of the spring term she signed with the Eileen Ford modeling agency in New York. By the time Candy came back to school, she was following in her mother's footsteps. She appeared in ads for Revlon's new cosmetic line, Tawny. She ignored the jokes of other students who called her "Tawny," and used the money to pursue her photographic interests.

Candice signed a contract with the Eileen Ford modeling agency. This photograph was taken for her modeling portfolio in 1966.

Candice earned money as a model to enable her to pursue a career in photojournalism.

She did not pursue her schoolwork as eagerly. She got an F in an art class and an F in opera, and a letter from the university asking her to leave. The Homecoming Queen asked to leave? Candy was stunned.

It didn't take long to get over the rejection. Before she had even left Penn, the **director** Sidney Lumet asked her to be in his new film *The Group*. By then, Candy was making $1,000 a day as a model. She never depended on her father for financial support again. So it was goodbye, college; hello, movies. This development shocked her parents. Not only was their precious daughter giving up college, but her first role in a film was of a lesbian! Realizing that she was now an adult, her parents let her make her own choices.

When the film came out, Candy got her first taste of critical reviews. In a *Life* magazine article called "A Goddess Upstages the Girls," the writer Pauline Kael called Candy a "golden lioness of a girl" who "doesn't appear interested enough even to stay awake." Kael went on to say that Candy's "only flair for acting is in her nostrils." This last comment would become the most quoted line about Candy's acting in her career and take a long time to overcome.

But no mere critic could stop her from making movies. Once her career had begun, it took off like a rocket.

Nobody's Dummies

After her film debut, Candy told reporters she wanted to succeed "as a person, not as an actress." She was called "candid" and "outspoken" for this statement. Her love life and social life both suffered. "Men seemed to want me to be more than I was," she remembered, "and women to want me to be less."

Edgar Bergen celebrated with his daughter after Candice signed a six-year contract with Columbia Pictures.

At 19, she was swept off her feet by a 37-year-old Austrian count, but she found his group of European socialites to be empty and sad. She quickly made another film, *The Sand Pebbles,* with Steve McQueen, in Hong Kong and other Asian locations. An actor in the film, Richard Attenborough, told her over dinner of his desire to make a film about the life of Mahatma Gandhi of India. He wanted Candy to play her idol, Margaret Bourke-White, in the film.

More films in foreign locations followed—*The Day the Fish Came Out,* in Greece, and *Live for Life*, in France. When she returned to the United States in 1967 after being away for two years, Candy found it "chaotic, often unrecognizable." The fashions were strange, the country was in turmoil over the war in Vietnam, and **hippies** were everywhere. Candice spent her twenty-first birthday in Los Angeles, inviting family and friends to join her as she watched a screening of her favorite childhood film, *Snow White*. Where was her Magic Kingdom?

Shortly after her birthday party, Candice went to a party given by her old boyfriend, Terry Melcher. Melcher had become a big music producer, working with top rock groups like the Byrds. Before long, Candy had moved in with Terry. She convinced her parents she was still maintaining an apartment in New York, however. She didn't want them to know she was living with Terry. Though she felt like an outsider, Candy was soon spending her time with the music business leaders of the "counterculture." A purple house in Bel Air owned by John and Michelle Philips of the Mamas and the Papas was a favorite hangout. She experimented with drugs and didn't make another movie for a year.

Terry, she learned, liked to live "on the edge." When he got involved with a **cult** leader named Charles Manson, Candice was frightened. She and Terry moved to Malibu, and Terry became heavily involved with drugs and alcohol. Then the actress Sharon Tate and three others were found brutally murdered by Manson and his followers. Candice was convinced she could just as easily have been killed by this dangerous group. This time she was the one who left Terry.

While spending time with Terry, Candice had gone back to photojournalism, working for *Cosmopolitan* and *Esquire* magazines. A 12-page play she wrote in college was published, and she got her first royalty check, for $6.75. With Terry out of her life, though, making movies seemed like the thing to do. She filmed *The Magus* with Anthony Quinn and Michael Caine on the island of Majorca but felt awkward and incompetent in her acting role.

Candice was working as a photojournalist when she attended the Democratic National Convention in 1976.

She realized her looks alone couldn't carry her much longer. Making *Getting Straight* in Oregon was easier. It was about a student revolution on a college campus. After *The Adventurers*, based on a Harold Robbins novel, she wanted to change her screen image. She played a gutsy woman in *Soldier Blue*, one of the first films sympathetic to Native Americans.

While Candice was making film after film, the career of Edgar Bergen and Charlie McCarthy had faded. They had hosted a daytime **TV quiz show** called *Do You Trust Your Wife?* in 1956, but in the 1960s Edgar was reduced to playing county fairs. He even began appearing as a character actor *without* Charlie in films. Candice starred in three films in 1970: *Carnal Knowledge*, *The Hunting Party*, and *T. R. Baskin*. Edgar, meanwhile, had only a tiny cameo appearance that year in *The Phynx*. Times had really changed.

Because of his sudden lack of popularity and her new success, Edgar and Candy's relationship became strained. Actually, Candy found that she wasn't getting along with either of her parents. Her mother had been known in the past as "Edgar Bergen's wife." Now she was "Candice Bergen's mother." And Candice's choice of boyfriends had not improved much. She bought her childhood dream house, the Aviary, where Katharine Hepburn had lived, but there was no Prince Charming to share it with her. She began dating the producer Bert Schneider. Their relationship lasted for a couple of years; during that time he got her involved with radical political and social causes. Eventually Candice found that being with him was riskier for her than being with Terry Melcher. Schneider announced that he wanted to have affairs with several

Candice's career began to take off when Edgar's began to decline, and this caused a strain on their relationship.

different women *while* he was with Candy. "Free love," as this style of living was called, had become popular among some groups at the time. Candy told him goodbye.

Schneider made one major contribution, however. One night as Candice feuded with her father on the phone, Schneider told her to tell Edgar she loved him. She did. After a pause, Edgar said, "I love you, too, Monstro." Perhaps fittingly, he had used his pet name for her—the name of the whale in the Disney masterpiece *Pinocchio*. Pinocchio was the wooden- puppet boy who wanted to be human. Amazingly, it was the first time either of them had told the other, "I love you."

Candice is shown here arriving at the Academy Awards in 1973.

By the time she was 25, Candice had been in 11 movies. The actor Gene Hackman, with whom she did two films, taught her to respect acting. She did better work, as in *The Wind and the Lion* with Sean Connery, though nothing, she felt, was extraordinary. As a photojournalist, she traveled the world photographing and writing about major celebrities like the film legend Charlie Chaplin. She did photo-essays for NBC's *Today* morning TV show. She hosted *Saturday Night Live* three times its first year. But something was missing.

At the age of 30, Candice began to reassess her life and pay more attention to family and friends. She visited her old governess, Dee, who had moved to Missouri. She longed for true romance, with the man of her dreams. After her father turned 75 in 1978 and seemed to grow old almost overnight, Candy spent nearly a year in Los Angeles, just being near her original Prince Charming.

Their time together must have encouraged Edgar. His ill health improved. He decided to announce his retirement in the summer of 1978 and do a farewell performance in September at Caesars Palace in Las Vegas. It was like old times. Once again, after 60 years in show business, Edgar Bergen and Charlie McCarthy played to sold-out audiences. Amazing his family, Edgar performed the routines flawlessly, giving no hint of old age or illness. The reviews of the show the first three nights were unanimously enthusiastic. Then, after performing equally well for a fourth night, Edgar went to bed and died peacefully, in his sleep. It was two weeks before the seventeenth birthday of his son, Kris.

Jim Henson, the creator of the Muppets, gave a eulogy at the funeral. In creating Kermit the Frog, Henson had been inspired by Edgar, whose last film appearance was in *The Muppet Movie*. When the movie was released in 1979, it was dedicated to Edgar Bergen. And Charlie McCarthy went on display at the Smithsonian Institution in Washington, D.C. Charlie had become a national treasure.

When Candy took another film role, it was comedic, just as her father had suggested so many years ago. In *Starting Over* with Jill Clayburgh, Candice's truly awful singing was hilarious. The critics said she had come of age as an actress. She was nominated for an Academy Award for best supporting actress.

Still, her father was gone and there was a hole in her life. Personal and professional fulfillment was still missing. She would find both soon enough. One would come from a French film director named Louis Malle, and the other from a sharp-tongued character named Murphy Brown.

From Belly Talk to Belly Laughs

On July 4, 1975, Candice was invited to a party in Connecticut given by the director Mike Nichols and his wife, Annabel. There Candy met French film director Louis Malle, the maker of films like *The Lovers* and *Murmur of the Heart*. Seated next to Malle, Candice found him to be "brave, brilliant, gifted and daring." But Candice, who had met some of the top celebrities in the world, found herself too intimidated by Malle's reputation to even speak.

In the next few years, her college buddy Mary Ellen Mark often told her that Louis Malle was the perfect man for her.

Candice Bergen met Louis Malle four years before she married him in 1979.

Candice ignored the advice until the winter of 1979, when Louis called her in New York City and invited her to lunch. Oddly, Candice had unexpectedly thought of him just the night before. They had lunch at the famous Russian Tea Room the next day. The conversation lasted until dinnertime. They talked "about film, their families, painting, travel, relationships, politics." Many dates followed, including one to celebrate Candice's thirty-fourth birthday. They spent that summer together at a house on Long Island, New York. Louis's children from previous relationships—his son, Cuote, and his daughter, Justine—came along. Candice said in *Knock Wood* that she "had never felt happier, fuller times than those we spent that summer, reading Doctor Seuss, seeing *Superman*, composing notes to the Tooth Fairy, picking strawberries, catching crabs."

That September she and Louis married in a small country ceremony at Lugagnac, Louis's hometown in France. Candice's mother and brother and members of Louis's family attended. Charlie's sister had finally found her prince, and a new Magic Kingdom all her own.

In 1981 Candice turned in another fine comedy performance in *Rich and Famous*. Once again, the "new" Candice Bergen was well received by the critics. The next year, she played Margaret Bourke-White in *Gandhi* for its director Richard Attenborough, 15 years after he had suggested she play the part.

Candice played the sorceress Morgan le Fay in the three-hour CBS movie *Arthur the King* in 1982. She appeared in *Stick* with Burt Reynolds in 1985. She even promoted her own line of perfume—Cie—but it was obvious that Candice had other priori-

Candice joined Louis in Paris when he won three Cesar Awards for his film, *Au Revoir Les Enfants*.

ties in the early 1980s. Her new family was her focus. As she told a reporter for *Cosmopolitan* magazine in 1993, "when a miracle comes along, you have to grab it."

Her new happiness made Candice reflective of her life. She decided to write a book. Her memoir, *Knock Wood*, was published in April 1984. It was a main selection of the Literary Guild book club the month it came out. The book finally put to rest any rumors that she had used a **ghost writer** for all her magazine articles. Yes, it was true. Candice Bergen had not only beauty but brains, too.

In February 1985 Candice acted in the **TV miniseries** *Hollywood Wives*. She did another TV movie, *Murder: By Reason of Insanity*. That fall another miracle arrived in her life. This one would make her even more devoted to family life. Nine-pound 2-ounce Chloe Malle was born on November 8, 1985.

Candice appeared in the CBS movie *The Mayflower Madam* in November 1987 as good-girl-gone-bad Sydney Biddle Barrows, but otherwise she was not getting that many job offers. It brought to mind the old Hollywood saying "Out of sight, out of mind." One script she got thrilled her, however. It was the "pilot" script for a potential new TV series called *Murphy Brown*. (A pilot script is a tryout; if it's successful, more episodes are produced.) Candice made her first in-flight phone call to tell the show's creators how much she loved the script. Husband-and-wife-team Diane English and Joel Shukovsky thought Candice was perfect to play the tough-minded, sharp-tongued TV news show journalist.

Unfortunately, Kim LeMasters, president of CBS Entertainment, did not agree. He didn't think Candice could do the role. And when she auditioned in front of network executives, the reading went terribly. Diane English, though, insisted that Candice be given the role. English was wise. The year the show first aired—1988—Candice won an Emmy for outstanding lead actress in a comedy series. She won again in 1989, 1990 and 1994. *Murphy Brown* became one of the most popular comedy TV series of all time. In 1991 the show's episodes about the pregnancy—the episodes Vice President Dan Quayle discussed—were both number one in their time slot.

Candice absolutely loved playing Murphy Brown. "It was always a dream to do comedy," she told *People* magazine in 1991. "This is the one area of acting where I ever felt passion, confidence and joy."

Candice cracks up with the cast on the set of *Murphy Brown.*

Remember that letter she got from the University of Pennsylvania—the one asking her to leave? Well, in 1992 the university asked her back, so they could give her an honorary doctor of law's degree.

Candice's career is not the only one in the family that has made great strides since their marriage. Louis Malle's foreign films have been nominated for six Academy Awards. But, like his wife, he prefers spending time with his family to making movies. These days, he, Candice, Chloe, his college-age kids, Justine and Cuote, and their cats—Pearl and Lucy—are often together at their homes in California, New York, and France.

In addition to being seen each week as Murphy Brown, Candice is the national spokeswoman for the U.S. Sprint long-distance telephone company. In 1993 she was voted Spokesperson of the Year for her work with U.S. Sprint.

Awards and recognition for the Bergens keep rolling in. The December 1993 cover of *Smithsonian* magazine was of Charlie McCarthy. "Grand master of the snappy comeback," read the caption. One month before, the board of directors of the Hollywood Entertainment Museum held their fifth annual Hollywood Legacy Awards ceremony, to recognize contributions to the film industry. The Bergen family, represented by Candice, her brother (now a successful film editor), and her mother were there to accept the honor.

It was enough to make Dan Quayle smile. In a Hollywood community where the divorce rate is high and children of famous people often grow up unhappy and without love, a fairy princess from Bel Air turned out just fine. Bright, beautiful Candice Bergen has triumphed as an actress, author, model, photojournal-

Candice answers questions from the audience after receiving the Jack Benny Award for achievement in comedy in 1993.

ist and—most important, as far as she's concerned—a *mom*. From photojournalism to comedy, she's done it all with remarkable grace and good humor. It's easy to see that "Charlie's sister" was never a dummy, after all. And, in looking back to discover the secret of her success, one can only form a single conclusion: It must have been those family values.

Glossary

Academy Awards Annual awards given since 1927 to film artists and technicians by the Academy of Motion Picture Arts and Sciences. The gold-plated Oscar statuettes awarded by the Academy recognize excellence in filmmaking.

Broadway A street in New York City famous for its theaters.

cult Any group of people bound together by devotion to a person, belief system, or set of practices.

Democrat A member of the Democratic political party in the United States, typically characterized by a belief in civil rights and trust in big government.

director The person who oversees the making of a motion picture. A director's major task is to guide the actors in their roles.

dummy A small representation of a human used by ventriloquists as a performing "partner." The term is also slang for a person who is silent by nature or physical disadvantage or who is not very smart.

Emmy Award An award given annually by the National Academy of Television Arts and Sciences. The Emmy recognizes excellence in performances, production, and programming.

Enchanted Forest A name for a forest in a fairy-tale land.

governess A woman hired to educate and train children in a private household (not in a school).

ghost writer A person who writes for another person but doesn't get public credit for the work. Famous people sometimes use ghost writers to help them create a book about their lives.

hippies People, especially of the late 1960s, who rejected established social customs and values. Supposedly the hippies were trying to become more aware of themselves, but often they took illegal drugs and lived irresponsibly.

44

Jack Benny Award An award given annually by students at the University of California at Los Angeles (UCLA). Comedian Jack Benny's daughter was a founder of this award, which recognizes excellence in the field of comedy.

Magic Kingdom A fairy tale-like setting, such as the land in the movie *Snow White*.

photojournalist A person who combines writing and photography in essays for publication.

Prince Charming The prince who falls in love with Snow White in the Disney film *Snow White*. The term Prince Charming may also refer to a person's ideal romantic love.

Republican A member of the Republican political party in the United States. Republicans typically favor big business and distrust big government.

script A paper that describes, scene by scene, what takes place in a film.

TV miniseries A lengthy movie made for television that spans four hours or more and is usually broadcast in two or more parts on successive evenings.

TV quiz show A television program on which contestants answer questions and win prizes.

vaudeville Theatrical entertainment popular at the beginning of the twentieth century that consists of individual performances by acrobats, comedians, dancers, magicians, singers, ventriloquists, and others.

ventriloquism The art of speaking with little or no lip movement so that the voice appears to be coming from some other source, such as a ventriloquist's dummy.

ventriloquist ("vent") One who performs ventriloquism.

Index

46